# the Cereal Lover's Cookbook

# the Cereal Lover's Cookbook

FUN, EASY RECIPES FOR EVERY
OCCASION, MADE WITH YOUR
FAVORITE READY-TO-EAT CEREALS

## LAUREN CHATTMAN

PHOTOGRAPHY BY DUANE WINFIELD

 JOHN WILEY & SONS, INC.

FOOD STYLING BY MEGAN FAWN SCHLOW
PROP STYLING BY GERRI WILLIAMS
BOOK DESIGN BY DEBORAH KERNER • DANCING BEARS DESIGN

Library of Congress Cataloging-in-Publication Data:

Chattman, Lauren.
  The cereal lover's cookbook : fun, easy recipes for every occasion, made with your
favorite ready-to-eat cereals / Lauren Chattman ; photography by Duane Winfield.
      p. cm.
  Includes index.
  ISBN-13 978-0-7645-9774-9 (cloth : alk. paper)
  ISBN-10 0-7645-9774-4 (cloth : alk. paper)
  1. Cookery (Cereals) I. Title.
  TX808.C43 2006
  641.6'31–dc22
                          2005013733

# Contents

# Acknowledgments

Thanks first of all to Justin Schwartz, who brought this idea to me and helped me make it a book. His enthusiasm for all things cereal was inspiring. Christine DiComo helped move the project along from start to finish. Copyeditor Amy Handy made sure every t was crossed. I was delighted to have Duane Winfield work his photo magic on my recipes. As always, he captured on film the fun I had making this food. Thanks also to Megan Fawn Schlow for her expert food styling and Gerri Williams for colorful prop styling. I had admired several of Deborah Kerner's book designs, so when I heard she would be designing this one, I was so happy. As always, Angela Miller was around for excellent advice and entertaining conversation. And thanks to Jack, Rose, and Eve for eating cereal for breakfast, lunch, and dinner and loving it.

# Introduction

## The Modest Origins and Spectacular Rise of Ready-to-Eat Cereal

Until the end of the 19th century, if you wanted a bowl of cereal for breakfast, you had to boil some wheat, rice, corn, or oats for hours or even overnight before it became a mush soft enough to eat. Ready-to-eat cereal as we know it was created by American Seventh-Day Adventists in the 1890s during their search for bland, high-fiber, vegetarian foods that they believed would promote healthy digestion and curb "unhealthy" desires, leading the way to physical and mental well-being. At an Adventist sanitarium run by his brother Dr. John Kellogg in Battle Creek, Michigan, Will Kellogg accidentally invented cereal flakes when he overcooked a pot of boiled wheat and tried to salvage it by pressing it into crackers, only to wind up with dried bits and pieces. He tentatively served the flakes with milk, and to his great surprise the new dish was a hit with patients. Over the next few years the Kellogg brothers experimented with preparing other grains this way, making oat flakes, rice flakes, and corn flakes in the sanitarium kitchen. If ever there was an unpromising start to a billion-dollar industry, this has to be it!

John and Will Kellogg were indeed slow to see the potential of cereal flakes. For the first few years they were made, the flakes were only available for sale through the sanitarium's store, which dispensed patent medicines to outpatients. Who knows what we'd all be eating for breakfast if C. W. Post, an inventor and entrepreneur, had not checked into the Battle Creek facility after one of his many nervous collapses. Post was so impressed with the business possibilities of the "health foods" served to him that when he checked out he opened up his own sanitarium and test kitchen in Battle Creek and developed Postum®, a caffeine-free coffee substitute, which he marketed not just to his patients but to the general public as a drink that would "make the blood red" rather than sap moral energy, as coffee reputedly did.

But even Post, a visionary who saw the potential of national advertising in promoting his health foods, was at first unimpressed with packaged cereal per se. His next product, Grape-Nuts®, was only marketed as a cereal in 1897 when it failed to catch on as a grain beverage. After Post's success selling Grape-Nuts as a breakfast food, Will Kellogg finally ventured into the marketplace with Kellogg's® Corn Flakes® in 1906. Emboldened by the public's enthusiasm, he dreamt up Rice Krispies® several years later. The rest is cereal history.

In the last 100 years, ready-to-eat cereal has moved from the fad food fringe to the very center of the American diet. Today the average American eats an average of 10 pounds, or 160 bowls, of cereal per person per year. Almost half of us begin the day with cereal. It is hard to overstate the importance of cereal to the economy. It generates billions of dollars in sales each year and is the third most popular item sold at supermarkets after soda and milk.

Cereal is a cultural as well as economic force. C. W. Post led the way by making sure the whole country, and not just a local audience, saw newspaper advertisements for Grape-Nuts. His success prompted cereal marketers to think big. Early on, manufacturers linked their products with radio and television characters (Cheerios® sponsored the Lone Ranger radio program in the 1940s), gathered celebrity endorsements (Wheaties® has put a revered athlete on its box since 1934), or created cartoon characters of their own (Tony the Tiger™, Cap'n Crunch®), making cereal advertising a form of popular entertainment. The cereal business developed in tandem with mass advertising, and because of this, cereal has become part of our collective unconscious, something that unites us as a nation.

## Where Cereal Lovers Meet

The cult of cereal is both widespread and elusive. If you love cereal, you are one of many millions. But you may also feel alone with your bowl and spoon. Clubs for cereal enthusiasts have not popped up the way, say, clubs for people who love cocker spaniels can be found in every corner of country. That's absurd, don't you think?

The Internet provides one space where cereal lovers can meet and discuss their past and present favorites, swap recipes, and argue the relative merits of Froot Loops® and Fruity Pebbles®. At www.emptybowl.com, you will find forums for such discussions, as well as reviews of new products, with titles like "Reduced Sugar Cocoa Puffs: Dancing with the Devil?" Delicious!

An exciting new development for people who want to bring cereal out of the home and into the public is Cereality, a growing chain of cereal bars and cafes. At locations in Arizona and Pennsylvania, with more to open in the coming months and years, servers wear pajamas instead of the usual polyester fast-food uniforms. Not only is there a vast array of cereals to choose from but also a selection of milks—full-fat, skim, soy, chocolate—and toppings. You can design your own cereal parfait, choose from a variety of baked goods made from cereal, or just enjoy bowl after bowl of your favorite. If cereal is your life, log onto www.cereality.com for job opportunities and information on managing a franchise of your own.

A while ago, I came across an account of something called "Cereal Dating Nights" at the Westfield's chain of supermarkets in Australia. Recognizing the popularity of cereal and its conversation value among its single customers, Westfield's has invited them to cruise the cereal aisle every Monday night from 7 P.M. until closing, to pick up a favorite cereal and perhaps someone to go along with it. Maybe it's an idea to drop into your supermarket's suggestion box.

Let the nutritionists, economists, and sociologists analyze the merits and meanings of cereal in American life. This book is simply a celebration of a national favorite. Most Americans love cereal for one reason: We can count on it. A lot has been written about comfort foods like rice pudding and mashed potatoes, but ready-to-eat cereal is the ultimate security blanket. When there's no time to cook and there's nothing else to eat, it's always there. Whether you're a natural foods fanatic or a sugar fiend, there's a box of cereal to suit your taste. You probably grew up eating it, so it makes you feel like a kid again. Why not use this convenience food to build other dishes that are simple to make and pleasing to a range of eaters? This book does just that, extending the usefulness of some favorite cereals by incorporating them into quick and delicious dishes for breakfast, lunch, dinner, and dessert.

## Thinking Outside the Bowl

For years, people have been pushing the envelope a bit to see what cereal can do in combination with ingredients aside from milk, and at meals other than breakfast. I don't know who was the first person to stir corn flake crumbs into meatloaf or add All-Bran® to muffin batter, but I do know that since then creative cooks in corporate test kitchens and at home have been dreaming up ways to use America's favorite convenience food in fun and easy dishes for every meal and occasion. Cereal just begs to be used in cooking, for several reasons:

It's there. If you are a typical American, you probably have several boxes of cereal in your pantry right now. Why not use what you have to cook dinner tonight? No bread crumbs for meatloaf? You can always use Wheaties. No flour for brownies? Crushed Cocoa Krispies® can be used in a pinch.

It adds texture and flavor to foods. Cereal is not just an ingredient for the desperate and disorganized (although it can certainly work for you if you are!). It brings texture and flavor to all kinds of dishes. Oven-Crisped Chicken Breasts wouldn't taste half as good if they used bread crumbs instead of corn flakes. Peach shortcakes made with Frosted Flakes® have a delicate crunch that plain baking powder biscuits will never have.

It's fun. As I was developing the recipes for this book, my family and I played a little game called "Guess what cereal I used today?" If you want to amaze people, bake up a batch of Cap'n Crunch Sour Cream Corn Muffins, let everyone enjoy the sweet corn flavor, and then ask them to guess the secret ingredient. Bringing tabbouleh made with Grape-Nuts instead of bulgur to the next potluck picnic is a sure way to get the conversation going. For some kids, the definition of fun is cooking with a combination of cereal and marshmallows. So go ahead and enjoy.

## Getting Ready to Cook

Boxed cereal is by definition a convenience food. There's not much you need to do with it before you start to cook. Some of the recipes in this book call for whole cereal. Simply measure out the cereal with a dry measuring cup and proceed. Other recipes call for crushed cereal. For the sake of accuracy and simplicity, I call for measuring the cereal before crushing it. Then there's no chance of winding up with too much crushed cereal and throwing away the extra, or winding up with too little and having to crush more, tablespoonful by tablespoonful, until you have the right amount. What's the best way to crush cereal? Small quantities can be placed in a small zipper-lock bag. Use your palm or a rolling pin to crush it into crumbs. Larger quantities can also be crushed this way, or can be ground fine in a food processor fitted with a metal blade.

## Storing Cereal

One of the great things about cereal is its long shelf life. Take a look at the sell-by date on any box in the supermarket, and you will be amazed at the many months, and sometimes even years, that a manufacturer will guarantee the freshness of its product. It's important, however, to take steps to preserve cereal's freshness and crunch once the box is opened. Moisture is the bane of boxed cereal, so it's especially important if you live in a humid climate to protect opened cereal from it. If you are going to go through it quickly (less than one week), taking care to roll closed the bag inside the box and storing the box on a shelf in the pantry is fine. If you think it will take you several weeks to finish a box, transfer the cereal to an airtight container or zipper-lock bag and store at room temperature. For longer storage, I keep my cereal in airtight containers in the refrigerator or freezer, where it will stay fresh and crisp indefinitely and will be handy when I need a half-cup here or a few tablespoons there.

## Substituting Cereals

Every name-brand cereal I can think of (with the notable exception of Grape-Nuts) has an equivalent made by a competing brand, not to mention countless generic and supermarket-brand equivalents. If a recipe calls for crispy rice cereal, you may use brand name Kellogg's Rice Krispies, or you may certainly use the warehouse club crisp rice cereal instead if you like. Beyond these substitutions, it's possible to substitute a cereal with similar flavor and texture properties in a recipe for the sake of convenience or variety. Let common sense guide you, and then feel free to experiment. Try Special K®, a flaked oat cereal, in place of Wheaties, a flaked wheat cereal, in Crisp Turkey Cutlets with Cranberry Pan Sauce. Or use Fruity Pebbles instead of Froot Loops in Chewy Froot Loop Squares if you like.

# the Cereal Lover's Cookbook

# breakfast

Sure, you can just pour it into a bowl and add milk, but you can also use cereal to make muffins, scones, waffles, pancakes, quick breads, and scrambled egg dishes. Some highlights: Jam-Filled Streusel Muffins made with Grape-Nuts, Crunchy Cornflake-Almond French Toast, and Migas with Corn Chex®, Jack Cheese, and Chorizo.

# cap'n crunch sour cream corn muffins

Who knew that this kid's favorite could be an easy way to add great corn flavor to baked goods when you don't have corn meal in the pantry? These can easily be varied. For Bacon-Corn Muffins, add ¼ cup crumbled crisp-cooked bacon to the ingredients listed below. For Blueberry-Lemon Muffins, add ¾ cup washed and stemmed blueberries and ½ teaspoon grated lemon zest.

2 cups all-purpose flour

1 ½ teaspoons baking powder

1 teaspoon baking soda

½ teaspoon salt

4 cups Cap'n Crunch, finely crushed
(about 1 ½ cups crumbs)

1 cup milk, or more if necessary

¾ cup sour cream

2 large eggs

6 tablespoons (¾ stick) unsalted butter,
melted and cooled

1. Preheat the oven to 400°F. Line a 12-cup muffin tin with paper liners or coat it with cooking spray.

2. In a small bowl, combine the flour, baking powder, baking soda, and salt.

3. In a large bowl, combine the Cap'n Crunch crumbs, milk, sour cream, eggs, and melted butter and stir until smooth. Add the flour mixture, stirring until just combined. If the mixture is too dry, stir in more milk, 1 tablespoon at a time, until it is a very thick batter, but all the dry ingredients are moistened.

4. Fill each cup until it is full. Bake the muffins until they are set and golden on top, 16 to 18 minutes. Let the muffins cool in the pan for about 5 minutes, invert them onto a wire rack, and then turn them right side up on the rack to cool completely. The muffins will keep in an airtight container at room temperature for 2 days.

# jam-filled streusel muffins

Grape-Nuts combined with chopped nuts is an unbeatable streusel muffin topping. A little jam in the center is a sweet surprise.

**STREUSEL TOPPING**

1/3 cup Grape-Nuts

1/3 cup pecans or walnuts, coarsely chopped

1/3 cup light brown sugar

1/2 teaspoon ground cinnamon

3 tablespoons unsalted butter, melted

**MUFFINS**

2 cups unbleached all-purpose flour

1 tablespoon baking powder

1/2 teaspoon salt

1/2 cup (1 stick) unsalted butter, melted and cooled

2/3 cup granulated sugar

2 large eggs

1 teaspoon vanilla extract

1 cup whole or low-fat milk

1/4 cup best-quality fruit preserves

1. Preheat the oven to 375°F. Line a 12-cup muffin tin with paper liners or coat it with cooking spray.
2. Make the Streusel Topping: In a small mixing bowl, combine the Grape-Nuts, nuts, brown sugar, and cinnamon. Stir in the melted butter to form coarse crumbs. Place the bowl in the freezer until ready to use.
3. Make the Muffins: In a medium mixing bowl, combine the flour, baking powder, and salt.
4. In a large mixing bowl, whisk together the melted butter, granulated sugar, eggs, vanilla, and milk. With a wooden spoon, stir in the flour mixture until just combined.
5. Fill each cup about half full. Spoon 1 teaspoon of preserves on top of the batter.

*(continued on page 6)*

Cover the preserves with more batter so that each muffin cup is about ¾ full. Remove the streusel from the freezer. Scatter the crumbs evenly over the muffins and press on the topping lightly with your fingers so that it will adhere to the muffins.

6. Bake the muffins until they are golden, 18 to 20 minutes. Let the muffins cool in the pan for about 5 minutes, invert them onto a wire rack, and then turn them right side up on the rack to cool completely. These muffins will keep in an airtight container at room temperature for up to 2 days.

# whole wheat muffins with figs and pecans

Adding Wheaties to muffin batter is a great way to add whole-grain flavor and
nutrition without weighing the muffins down. Look for soft, moist dried figs at the
market (other dried fruits such as raisins, chopped prunes, or chopped apricots may
be substituted).

3 cups Wheaties

1 cup all-purpose flour

²/₃ cup light brown sugar

¼ cup whole wheat flour

1 ½ teaspoons baking powder

¾ teaspoon baking soda

½ teaspoon salt

½ teaspoon ground cinnamon

Pinch ground nutmeg

1 ¼ cups buttermilk

1 large egg, beaten

¼ cup vegetable oil

1 cup dried figs, stemmed and coarsely chopped

½ cup pecans, finely chopped

1. Preheat the oven to 400°F. Line a 12-cup muffin tin with paper liners or coat it
   with cooking spray.
2. In a large mixing bowl, combine the Wheaties, flour, brown sugar, whole wheat
   flour, baking powder, baking soda, salt, cinnamon, and nutmeg. Stir to blend.
3. In another large mixing bowl, whisk together the buttermilk, egg, and oil. With a
   wooden spoon, stir in the flour mixture until just combined. Stir in the figs and
   pecans.
4. Fill each cup about ¾ full. Bake the muffins until they are set, 15 to 17 minutes.
   Let the muffins cool in the pan for about 5 minutes, invert them onto a wire rack,
   and then turn them right side up on the rack to cool completely. These muffins will
   keep in an airtight container at room temperature for up to 2 days.

# pumpkin-bran coffee cake

MAKES 12 SQUARES

This moist, not too sweet breakfast cake has cereal in both the cake and the topping.

6 tablespoons (¾ stick) unsalted butter

1¼ cup Bran Buds®

¼ cup pecans, finely chopped

1¼ cups firmly packed light brown sugar

1½ cups unbleached all-purpose flour

2 teaspoons baking powder

¼ teaspoon baking soda

1 teaspoon ground cinnamon

¼ teaspoon ground nutmeg

Pinch ground cloves

2 large eggs

1 cup canned pumpkin

1. Preheat the oven to 350°F. Spray an 8-inch-square baking pan with cooking spray. Melt 4 tablespoons of the butter and set aside. Cut the remaining 2 tablespoons of butter into small pieces.

2. In a medium bowl, combine ½ cup of the Bran Buds, the pecans, ¼ cup of the brown sugar, and the 2 cut-up tablespoons of butter and stir, mashing with the back of a spoon, to form bunches of crumbs. Place in the refrigerator while you make the batter.

3. In a small bowl, combine the flour, baking powder, baking soda, cinnamon, nutmeg, and cloves. In large bowl, whisk together the eggs, pumpkin, and the 4 tablespoons of melted butter until smooth. Stir in the flour mixture until just combined. Stir in the remaining ¾ cup of Bran Buds.

4. Scrape the batter into the prepared pan and smooth into an even layer with a spatula. Sprinkle the pecan mixture over the top of the batter. Bake for about 35 minutes, or until a toothpick inserted into the center of the cake comes out with just a few moist crumbs clinging to it. Transfer the pan to a wire rack to cool for 20 minutes and serve warm, or let cool completely.

# cinnamon-raisin bran scones

Adding raisin bran cereal to these scones gives them a wholesome, wheaty flavor and a light, cakey texture. No need to add fruit, since the raisins are packed right in the cereal box.

2 cups all-purpose flour

¼ cup sugar, plus 1 tablespoon for sprinkling

2 teaspoons baking powder

½ teaspoon salt

¼ teaspoon ground cinnamon

10 tablespoons (1¼ sticks) cold unsalted butter, cut into ¼-inch cubes

1½ cups raisin bran cereal

1 cup milk

1 large egg, lightly beaten

1. Preheat the oven to 450°F. Line a baking sheet with parchment paper or spray with cooking spray.
2. In a large mixing bowl, combine the flour, ¼ cup sugar, baking powder, salt, and cinnamon. Add the chilled butter pieces and, with an electric mixer, mix on low speed until the mixture resembles coarse meal. Stir in the raisin bran.
3. Stir in the milk on low speed until the dry ingredients are just moistened. Do not overmix.
4. Turn the dough onto a lightly floured work surface and divide it in half. Shape each half into a 6-inch disk. With a sharp chef's knife, cut each disk into 6 wedges. Place the wedges ½ inch apart on the prepared baking sheet. Brush the scones with the beaten egg and sprinkle them with the remaining tablespoon of sugar.
5. Bake the scones until they are golden, 12 to 14 minutes. Let them cool for 5 minutes and serve them warm, or let them cool completely. The scones are best eaten on the day they are baked.

# "brancakes" with maple-blueberry sauce

You will not believe how tall and fluffy these healthy pancakes are, considering that they're made with All-Bran cereal.

**MAPLE-BLUEBERRY SAUCE**

2 1/2 cups fresh or frozen blueberries

1/4 cup water

1/3 cup pure maple syrup

2 tablespoons molasses

**"BRANCAKES"**

1 cup All-Bran

1 cup all-purpose flour

2 tablespoons dark brown sugar

2 teaspoons baking powder

1/4 teaspoon baking soda

1/4 teaspoon salt

2 cups buttermilk

2 large eggs

4 tablespoons (1/2 stick) unsalted butter, melted and cooled

1. Make the Maple-Blueberry Sauce: In a small saucepan, combine 1 1/2 cups of the blueberries, the water, and maple syrup and bring to a boil. Turn down the heat to medium-low and simmer until the berries burst, stirring often, about 10 minutes. Stir in the remaining 1 cup of berries and continue to cook until the juices are thickened, another 7 to 10 minutes. Set aside, covering to keep warm. (The sauce can be made up to 3 days in advance. Refrigerate in an airtight container and reheat before serving.)

2. Make the "Brancakes": Place the All-Bran in the work bowl of a food processor or a blender and process until finely ground. Transfer to a large mixing bowl and stir in the flour, brown sugar, baking powder, baking soda, and salt.

3. In a medium bowl, whisk together the buttermilk, eggs, and melted butter. Pour into the bowl with the dry ingredients and stir with a wooden spoon until everything is moistened. Don't worry if there are some small lumps.

4. Spray the surface of a griddle or a large skillet with cooking spray, and heat it over

*(continued on page 13)*

medium-high heat. Test the griddle or skillet after a couple of minutes by drizzling a few drops of water onto the cooking surface. If the drops sizzle and evaporate, the surface is hot enough.

5. For each pancake, spoon or ladle about ¼ cup batter onto the surface and cook the pancake until the top begins to bubble and the bottom is golden, 2 to 3 minutes. Check occasionally to make sure the pancakes aren't cooking too quickly and adjust the heat if necessary. Flip each pancake and cook until it is golden on the second side, 1 to 2 minutes more. Serve immediately with Maple-Blueberry Sauce or keep warm in a preheated 200°F oven on a platter loosely covered with aluminum foil. Repeat with the remaining batter, removing the pan from the heat and spraying the cooking surface, if necessary, with more cooking spray before beginning each new batch.

## Corn Flakes: A HAPPY ACCIDENT AND THE BIRTH OF A CEREAL EMPIRE

Next time you ruin a pot of something or other by leaving it on the stove too long, think of Will Kellogg, who did just that with a pot of wheat he was preparing to serve to patients at his brother's sanitarium in Battle Creek, Michigan. Loath to waste food, he rolled the overcooked wheat into large, thin flakes. They were a great hit in the hospital dining room when served with milk. With a strong belief in the health properties of cereal products, Will and his brother Dr. John Kellogg experimented with creating flakes out of other types of grain. Flakes made from corn were the first to be packaged and put on the market under the Kellogg's brand name in 1906. Will Kellogg was also a precocious cereal marketer. In 1909, to boost sales of Kellog's® Corn Flakes, he pioneered the proof-of-purchases giveaway, offering anyone who bought a box a copy of Funny Jungleland Moving Pictures Booklet, which was available through Kellogg's for the next 23 years.

# crunchy cornflake-almond french toast

Serve with sliced strawberries and syrup on the side. For extra-rich French Toast, substitute ½ cup of heavy cream for the milk.

3 large eggs

1 cup milk

2 tablespoons sugar

1 teaspoon vanilla extract

½ teaspoon almond extract

⅛ teaspoon salt

2¾ cups cornflakes, lightly crushed

¾ cup sliced almonds, lightly crushed

2 tablespoons unsalted butter

8 slices firm white bread

1. Preheat the oven to 350°F. Lightly butter a rimmed baking sheet.
2. In a medium bowl, combine the eggs, milk, sugar, vanilla, almond extract, and salt and whisk until blended.
3. In a shallow bowl, combine the crushed cornflakes and almonds.
4. Melt ½ tablespoon of the butter in a large skillet over medium heat. Dip 2 slices of bread in the egg mixture, transfer to the bowl with the cornflake mixture, and coat the bread on both sides with the crumbs.
5. Cook the bread in the hot skillet until lightly crisped on both sides, 1 to 2 minutes per side, and transfer to the prepared baking sheet. Repeat with the remaining butter and bread.
6. Place the baking sheet in the oven and bake until the toast is deep golden, 10 to 15 minutes. Serve immediately.

# oatmeal-pecan waffles

These are good with maple syrup or apricot preserves.

1 cup unbleached all-purpose flour

1/2 cup quick-cooking or old-fashioned oats

3/4 cup pecans, finely chopped

1/4 cup firmly packed light brown sugar

1 1/2 teaspoons baking powder

1/4 teaspoon salt

1 1/2 cups whole or low-fat milk

1 large egg

1/4 cup (1/2 stick) unsalted butter, melted
   and cooled

1. In a large mixing bowl, stir together the flour, oats, pecans, brown sugar, baking powder, and salt.
2. Measure the milk into a large glass measuring cup. Crack the egg into the cup and beat lightly with a fork to break up the egg. Stir in the melted butter.
3. Pour into the mixing bowl and stir with a wooden spoon until everything is moistened. Don't worry if there are some small lumps.
3. Heat a waffle iron. Spray the grids with cooking spray.
4. Pour some batter (how much depends on the size of your waffle iron) onto the grids and spread it to the edges with a spatula. Cook the waffles until they are golden brown, 4 to 7 minutes, depending on your machine. Serve immediately.

# migas with corn chex, jack cheese, and chorizo

Chex cereal made with corn stands in for shredded strips of corn tortilla in this satisfying breakfast scramble. If you can't find chorizo, a spicy smoked sausage imported from Spain, use another smoked sausage that you like.

6 large eggs

¼ cup milk

¼ teaspoon salt

One 4-inch piece Spanish-style chorizo
   (about 3 ounces)

1 small yellow onion, finely chopped

1 cup Corn Chex

1 cup (3 ounces) shredded Monterey
   Jack or Cheddar cheese

2 tablespoons finely chopped cilantro

Tomato salsa (optional)

1. In a medium bowl, whisk together the eggs, milk, and salt and set aside.

2. Cut the chorizo into ½-inch-thick slices, then cut the slices into a ½-inch dice. Heat a nonstick skillet over medium heat and add the chorizo. Cook, stirring occasionally, until the fat is rendered and the chorizo is crispy, 2 to 3 minutes. Remove to a paper towel–lined plate and discard all but 1 tablespoon of fat from the pan.

3. Add the onion to the skillet and cook, stirring, until the onion has softened, 3 to 4 minutes. Add the Chex and cook, stirring, for 1 minute.

4. Add the egg mixture, the cheese, and cilantro to the skillet. Push the eggs around with a spatula, scraping up the cooked parts and allowing the liquid to flow to the bottom of the pan. Cook this way until the eggs are set, 2 to 3 minutes. Serve immediately, with tomato salsa on the side, if desired.

# froot loop and blueberry parfaits

This is a good way to sneak some fruit into a finicky kid's breakfast. It's also a fun breakfast after a slumber party.

1 cup fresh blueberries, picked over, washed, and dried

2 cups Froot Loops

Two 8-ounce containers low-fat vanilla yogurt

4 small strawberries, washed and stemmed (optional)

1. Gently toss the blueberries and Froot Loops in a medium bowl until well combined.
2. Beginning with a layer of yogurt, spoon alternate layers of yogurt and the Froot Loops mixture into each of 4 tall parfait glasses. Top each glass with a strawberry if desired.

### Yogurt and Cereal Parfaits

There are many ways to combine yogurt, fruit, and cereal to make breakfast parfaits for every taste. Use the quantities specified in Froot Loop and Blueberry Parfaits (above). Here are some suggestions to get you going:

❖ Cornflakes, vanilla yogurt, and strawberries

❖ Honey Nut Cheerios, vanilla yogurt, and grated apple mixed with sliced almonds

❖ Crumbled shredded wheat, raspberry yogurt, and fresh raspberries

❖ Frosted Flakes®, peach yogurt, and chopped fresh or dried apricots

❖ Crispy rice cereal, lemon yogurt, and diced fresh or canned pineapple

❖ Wheaties, plain yogurt, and bananas sprinkled with brown sugar

# honey-nut waffles

Try these with sliced bananas and a little bit of warmed honey on top. The unprocessed bran is optional, but it gives a nice texture to the waffles.

1 cup unbleached all-purpose flour

1 cup Honey Nut Cheerios®, finely crushed
 (about ½ cup crumbs)

½ cup unprocessed bran (optional)

½ cup finely chopped walnuts

2 teaspoons baking powder

¼ teaspoon salt

1 ½ cups whole or low-fat milk

2 large eggs

⅓ cup honey

¼ cup (½ stick) unsalted butter, melted
 and cooled

1. In a large mixing bowl, stir together the flour, crushed cereal, bran if using, nuts, baking powder, and salt in a large mixing bowl.

2. Measure the milk into a large glass measuring cup. Crack the eggs into the cup and beat lightly with a fork to break up the eggs. Stir in the honey and melted butter. Pour into the mixing bowl and stir with a wooden spoon until everything is moistened. Don't worry if there are some small lumps.

3. Heat a waffle iron. Spray the grids with cooking spray.

4. Pour some batter (how much depends on the size of your waffle iron) onto the grids and spread it to the edges with a spatula. Cook the waffles until they are golden brown, 4 to 7 minutes, depending on your machine. Serve immediately.

# cereal snacks, savory and sweet

Two cereal classics, savory cereal party mix and decadently sweet marshmallow treats, are the jumping-off points for this chapter, which also includes recipes for snack mixes such as Coconut-Curry and Apple Spice, and some cereal and marshmallow creations to suit fans of both Froot Loops and Raisin Bran.

# pecan-ginger party mix

The war horse recipe for cereal-based party mix can be spiced up considerably for various occasions. Here, ginger and pecans lend flavor to this sweet-and-salty snack. I like this around holiday time, as part of a larger spread of snacks with festive drinks. Improvising according to taste and the spices, nuts, and other add-ons you have on hand is easy once you know the basic formula.

6 cups mixed Chex cereals (rice, whole wheat, and corn)

2 cups small pretzels

2 cups pecan halves

4 tablespoons (½ stick) unsalted butter

2 tablespoons sugar

2 teaspoons salt

2 teaspoons ground ginger

¼ teaspoon cayenne

1. Preheat the oven to 250°F.
2. In a large mixing bowl, combine the Chex, pretzels, and pecan halves.
3. In a small saucepan over low heat, melt the butter. Whisk in the sugar, salt, ginger, and cayenne. Drizzle the mixture over the cereal, tossing to coat.
4. Spread the cereal mixture in an even layer in the bottom of a shallow roasting pan. Bake for 1 hour, stirring twice during baking. Transfer to a large bowl to cool completely. The party mix will keep in an airtight container at room temperature for 1 month.

# hot and spicy party mix

Good in the summertime, with cold beer before a barbecue or Mexican food.

6 cups mixed Chex cereals (rice, whole wheat, and corn)

2 cups small pretzels

2 cups salted peanuts

4 tablespoons (1/2 stick) unsalted butter

1 1/2 teaspoons salt

2 teaspoons sugar

2 teaspoons cayenne, or more to taste

1 1/2 teaspoons paprika

1. Preheat the oven to 250°F.
2. In a large mixing bowl, combine the Chex, pretzels, and peanuts.
3. In a small saucepan over low heat, melt the butter. Whisk in the salt, sugar, cayenne, and paprika. Drizzle the mixture over the cereal, tossing to coat.
4. Spread the cereal mixture in an even layer in the bottom of a shallow roasting pan. Bake for 1 hour, stirring twice during baking. Transfer to a large bowl to cool completely. The party mix will keep in an airtight container at room temperature for 1 month.

# coconut-curry party mix

MAKES ABOUT 10 CUPS

This party mix has a potent combination of Indian flavors—curry, coconut, raisins—that I find addictive.

6 cups mixed Chex cereals (rice, whole wheat, and corn)

2 cups whole almonds

1 1/2 cups small thin pretzels

1 cup sweetened flaked coconut

1/2 stick (1/4 cup) unsalted butter

1 tablespoon soy sauce

2 teaspoons curry powder

1/2 teaspoon cayenne

1/4 teaspoon salt

1 cup golden raisins

1. Preheat the oven to 250°F.
2. In a large mixing bowl, combine the Chex, almonds, pretzels, and coconut.
3. In a small saucepan over low heat, melt the butter. Whisk in the soy sauce, curry powder, cayenne, and salt. Drizzle the mixture over the cereal, tossing to coat.
4. Spread the cereal mixture in an even layer in the bottom of a shallow roasting pan. Bake for 1 hour, stirring twice during baking. Transfer to a large bowl to cool completely. Stir in the raisins. The party mix will keep in an airtight container at room temperature for 1 month.

## Custom Snack Mixes

Once you know the basic formula—6 cups cereal, 2 cups nuts, 2 cups pretzels, 4 tablespoons butter, 1½ teaspoons salt—it's easy to customize a cereal snack mix to your taste or improvise one with ingredients you have on hand. Here are a few ideas to get you thinking:

Japanese Restaurant Snack Mix: Use just Rice Chex. Substitute Wasabi peas for nuts and sesame sticks for pretzels. To season, add 1 tablespoon soy sauce, ¼ teaspoon salt, 2 teaspoons sugar, 1 teaspoon ground ginger, and ½ teaspoon garlic powder to the melted butter.

Kids' Favorite: Use honey-roasted peanuts. Substitute 1 cup goldfish crackers for 1 cup of the pretzels. To season, just add 2 teaspoons salt and 2 teaspoons sugar to the melted butter.

Thanksgiving Blend: Use walnuts. To season, add 2 teaspoons salt, 2 tablespoons maple syrup, and 1 teaspoon pumpkin pie seasoning to the melted butter. Add 1 cup dried cranberries to the cooled mix.

Tex-Mex: Use just Corn Chex. Substitute pumpkin seeds for the nuts. To season, add 2 teaspoons salt, 1 tablespoon light brown sugar, 1 teaspoon chili powder, and 1 teaspoon ground cumin to the melted butter.

# cereal lover's trail mix

This maple-scented mixture of oats, shredded wheat, and crispy rice cereal is a healthy and convenient snack-on-the-go and can also be served like granola, with milk or yogurt and fresh fruit.

3 cups old-fashioned (not quick-cooking) oats

1 cup spoon-size shredded wheat cereal

1 1/3 cups whole almonds

1 cup crispy rice cereal

1/4 cup honey

1/4 cup pure maple syrup

2 tablespoons molasses

2 tablespoons vegetable oil

1/2 teaspoon cinnamon

1/2 cup dried apples, coarsely chopped

1/2 cup raisins or dried cranberries

1. Preheat the oven to 300°F.

2. In a large bowl, combine the oats, shredded wheat, almonds, and crispy rice.

3. In a small saucepan, combine the honey, maple syrup, molasses, vegetable oil, and cinnamon. Heat over medium-low until warm, whisking. Pour over the cereal mixture and stir to coat.

4. Scrape the trail mix onto a rimmed baking sheet and spread into an even layer. Bake, stirring once or twice to prevent the trail mix on the edges from burning, until the trail mix is dry and toasted, 30 to 35 minutes. Remove from the oven and let cool completely on the baking sheet.

5. Transfer the cooled mixture to a large airtight container. Stir in the apples and raisins or cranberries. The trail mix will keep at room temperature in the airtight container for up to 2 weeks.

## Variation: Chocolate-Apricot Cereal Lover's Trail Mix

For a more candylike trail mix: Substitute honey for the maple syrup, 3/4 cup chopped dried apricots for the raisins, and add 1/2 cup semisweet chocolate chips to the cooled cereal mixture along with the fruit.

# maple-corn buttercrunch

Here's another addictive popcornlike snack, this one made with puffed corn cereal, maple syrup, and walnuts.

4 tablespoons (½ stick) unsalted butter, plus more for greasing the baking sheet and spoon

6 cups Kix®

1 cup walnut pieces, coarsely chopped

1 cup pure maple syrup

¼ teaspoon salt

1. Preheat the oven to 250°F. Butter a large rimmed baking sheet. Butter a wooden spoon.

2. In a large bowl, stir together the Kix and walnuts.

3. In a small, heavy saucepan, combine the butter, maple syrup, and salt. Bring to a boil and then lower the heat and simmer without stirring for 5 minutes.

4. Pour the mixture over the cereal and walnuts, stirring with the buttered wooden spoon until all the cereal is coated.

5. Scrape the mixture onto a rimmed baking sheet and press into an even layer. Bake, stirring several times to break up the cereal, until the mixture is toasted, about 45 minutes. Cool completely on the baking sheets, and then break up if necessary and transfer to an airtight container. This will keep in an airtight container at room temperature for 1 week.

# caramel-coated cheerios and peanuts

Here's a fun caramel-corn-and-peanut type mixture for snacking on at home while watching a movie or for taking out to the ball game.

6 cups plain Cheerios

1 cup Spanish peanuts

½ cup light brown sugar

¼ cup light corn syrup

2 tablespoons unsalted butter

1 tablespoon molasses

¼ teaspoon salt

1. Preheat the oven to 250°F.
2. In a large bowl, stir together the Cheerios and peanuts.
3. In a heavy saucepan, combine the brown sugar, corn syrup, butter, molasses, and salt. Bring to a boil and then lower the heat and simmer for 5 minutes, stirring frequently. Pour the mixture over the Cheerios and nuts, stirring with a wooden spoon until all the cereal is coated.
4. Scrape the mixture onto a rimmed baking sheet and press into an even layer. Bake, stirring several times to break up the cereal, until the mixture is toasted, about 45 minutes. Cool completely on the baking sheets, and then break up if necessary and transfer to an airtight container. This will keep in an airtight container at room temperature for 1 week.

# classic marshmallow squares

This is my favorite version of the classic. Butter and vanilla give these marshmallow treats richness and wholesome flavor.

3 tablespoons unsalted butter, plus more for
   greasing the pan
One 10-ounce package regular marshmallows

½ teaspoon vanilla extract
¼ teaspoon salt
4 cups crispy rice cereal

1. Line an 8-inch-square baking pan with heavy-duty aluminum foil, making sure that the foil is tucked into all the corners and that there is at least 1 inch overhanging the top of the pan on all sides. Lightly butter the bottom and sides of the foil-lined pan.

2. In a large saucepan over low heat, melt the butter. Add the marshmallows, vanilla, and salt and stir with a wooden spoon until melted. Remove the pan from the heat and stir in the crispy rice until evenly coated.

3. Turn the mixture into the prepared baking pan. Spray a rubber spatula with cooking spray and spread the mixture evenly across the pan. Let cool completely.

4. Grasping the overhanging foil on either side of the pan, lift out the marshmallow mixture and place it on a cutting board. Cut into 16 squares. These will keep, wrapped in plastic and at room temperature, for 2 to 3 days.

## Fun with Marshmallow Squares

I used to be happy just slicing my Marshmallow Squares into bars, but once I saw how the people in the Kellogg's kitchens used the mixture as an artistic medium, I wanted to try cutting, molding, and sculpting it into different shapes. Check out www.kelloggs.com for dozens of creative marshmallow treat ideas. Here are a few of my favorites:

Marshmallow Cutouts: Tint your marshmallow treats a pretty color by mixing a drop or two of food coloring into the marshmallows as they melt. Then spread the mixture onto a 12×15–inch buttered baking sheet. When cool, use cookie cutters to cut green treats into shamrocks, pink treats into hearts, orange treats into pumpkins, and so on. Cutouts may be embellished with frosting, and sprinkles and candy may be pressed into the frosting.

Marshmallow Squares Pizza: Make Classic Marshmallow Squares and press the mixture into a 9-inch-round buttered pan, making the outer edge a little bit higher than the inside of the round, to look like a pizza crust. When mixture is almost cool, scatter green sprinkles over it (to look like parsley) and place 1-inch circles of red fruit leather on top (to look like pepperoni).

Marshmallow Squares Kebabs: Thread 1-inch Marshmallow Squares onto skewers, alternating them with strawberries, whole marshmallows, and grapes.

Marshmallow Squares Ice Cream Sundaes: Press the warm Marshmallow Squares mixture into the bottoms and sides of buttered muffin cups. When cool, fill with a scoop of ice cream, top with chocolate or butterscotch sauce, whipped cream, and a maraschino cherry.

Marshmallow Squares "Gingerbread" House: A lot easier than baking gingerbread. Make a double batch of the treat mixture, divide, and press into two 12×15–inch buttered baking sheets. Turn one sheet out onto a large cutting board or platter to use as a base. Cut the other sheet to form the walls and roof of the house. Glue together the pieces with royal icing. Decorate with more icing, gumdrops, peppermints, and candy canes, as you would a real gingerbread house.

# chewy froot loop squares

Salted nuts cut the sweetness of the Froot Loops and marshmallows in this take on the classic cereal and marshmallow snack.

3 tablespoons unsalted butter, plus more for greasing the pan

One 10-ounce package regular marshmallows

2 cups crispy rice cereal

2 cups Froot Loops

¾ cup mixed salted nuts

1. Line an 8-inch-square baking pan with heavy-duty aluminum foil, making sure that the foil is tucked into all the corners and that there is at least 1 inch overhanging the top of the pan on all sides. Lightly butter the bottom and sides of the foil-lined pan.

2. In a large saucepan over low heat, melt the butter. Add the marshmallows and stir with a wooden spoon until melted. Remove the pan from the heat and stir in the crispy rice, Froot Loops, and nuts until evenly coated.

3. Turn the mixture into the prepared baking pan. Spray a rubber spatula with cooking spray and spread the mixture evenly across the pan. Let cool completely.

4. Grasping the overhanging foil on either side of the pan, lift the marshmallow mixture and place it on a cutting board. Cut into 16 squares. These will keep, wrapped in plastic and at room temperature, for 2 to 3 days.

# trail mix marshmallow squares

Made with raisin bran and sunflower or pumpkin seeds, these are chewier than the originals, and more wholesome-tasting for grown-ups, but with enough gooey marshmallow and chocolate to please the kids. Stir the chocolate chips in last, so that they don't completely melt before you get the mixture into the pan.

3 tablespoons unsalted butter, plus more for
   greasing the pan
One 10-ounce package regular marshmallows
½ teaspoon vanilla extract

¼ teaspoon salt
3 ½ cups raisin bran cereal
½ cup unsalted sunflower or pumpkin seeds
½ cup semisweet chocolate chips

1. Line an 8-inch-square baking pan with heavy-duty aluminum foil, making sure that the foil is tucked into all the corners and that there is at least 1 inch overhanging the top of the pan on all sides. Lightly butter the bottom and sides of the foil-lined pan.

2. In a large saucepan over low heat, melt the butter. Add the marshmallows, vanilla, and salt and stir with a wooden spoon until melted. Remove the pan from the heat and stir in the raisin bran and seeds.

3. Quickly stir in the chocolate chips and turn the mixture into the prepared baking pan. Spray a rubber spatula with cooking spray and spread the mixture evenly across the pan. Let cool completely.

4. Grasping the overhanging foil on either side of the pan, lift the marshmallow mixture and place it on a cutting board. Cut into 16 squares. These will keep, wrapped in plastic and at room temperature, for 2 to 3 days.

# salads, soups, and side dishes

In this chapter, cereal adds texture and flavor to dishes as diverse as Warm Spinach Salad with Bacon, Hard-Cooked Eggs, and Peppery Shredded Wheat; Corn and Potato Chowder with Crisped Bacon and Cornflake Topping; and Potato and Ham Gratin with Wheat and Bran Topping.

# warm spinach salad with bacon, hard-cooked eggs, and peppery shredded wheat

I love this salad because it contains so many elements of breakfast—bacon, eggs, shredded wheat—combined in a delicious salad suitable for brunch but also a light lunch or dinner.

1 cup spoon-size shredded wheat (unsweetened, not "frosted")

1 ½ tablespoons butter, melted

½ teaspoon coarsely and freshly ground black pepper, or more to taste

¼ teaspoon salt

6 ounces (about 8 cups) baby spinach, washed and dried

8 ounces bacon, cut into ½-inch pieces

½ medium red onion

1 small clove garlic, finely chopped

3 tablespoons balsamic vinegar

4 hard-boiled eggs, peeled and quartered lengthwise

1. Preheat the oven to 325°F.
2. In a medium bowl, combine the shredded wheat, melted butter, pepper, and salt and toss to combine. Spread the mixture onto a baking sheet, and bake, stirring once, until the shredded wheat is crisp and browned, about 12 minutes. Remove from the oven and let cool.
3. Place the spinach in a large salad bowl and set aside.
4. In a medium skillet over medium-high heat, fry the bacon, stirring occasionally, until crisp, about 10 minutes. Use a slotted spoon to remove it from the pan to a paper towel–lined plate. Pour the bacon fat into a heatproof measuring cup or bowl, and then return 3 tablespoons of it to the skillet. Discard any remaining fat.

(continued on page 44)

5. Add the onion to the skillet and cook, stirring frequently, until softened, about 3 minutes. Stir in the garlic and cook until fragrant, another minute. Stir in the vinegar, scraping the bottom of the pan to remove any browned bits.

6. Pour the warm dressing over the spinach and toss to coat. Add the bacon and toss again. Arrange the salad on four plates. Put 4 egg quarters on the perimeter of each plate. Sprinkle some of the peppery shredded wheat over each portion. Serve immediately.

# caesar salad with special K croutons

Special K cereal, toasted with garlic and olive oil, is transformed into delicious and healthy "croutons" for a cereal-lover's Caesar salad. For health reasons, I don't use raw eggs in my dressing, but the characteristic flavors of anchovy and parmesan cheese give this version the same great kick. Look for tender hearts of Romaine lettuce at your supermarket, or buy two larger Romaine lettuces and discard the tough outer leaves before using.

CROUTONS

1 tablespoon olive oil

1 clove garlic, peeled and lightly crushed

2 cups Special K

½ teaspoon salt

SALAD

6 tablespoons extra-virgin olive oil

2 tablespoons freshly squeezed lemon juice

1 teaspoon Worcestershire sauce

½ clove garlic, finely chopped

3 anchovy fillets, finely chopped

2 Romaine lettuce hearts, torn into bite-size pieces

½ cup freshly grated parmesan cheese

1. Make the Croutons: In a large skillet over medium heat, add the olive oil and garlic and cook, turning the garlic until it is lightly browned all over, 2 to 3 minutes. Remove the garlic clove and discard.

2. Add the Special K and salt to the skillet and cook, stirring, until the cereal is toasted and coated with oil, about 2 minutes. Transfer to a bowl to cool completely. (Cooled croutons will keep in an airtight container at room temperature for up to 1 week.)

3. Make the Salad: In a small bowl, whisk together the oil, lemon juice, Worcestershire sauce, garlic, and anchovies. Place the lettuce in a large bowl. Pour the dressing over the lettuce and toss to coat.

4. Add the parmesan cheese and the croutons to the bowl and toss again to distribute. Serve immediately.

## Sprinkling On the Cereal

For a lot of people, certain dishes are just an excuse to sprinkle on a buttery, golden-crispy bread crumb topping of crunchy croutons. Cereal flakes—Wheaties, cornflakes, Special K, bran flakes—sautéed in a little butter and seasoned with salt, pepper, and herbs and spices of your choice make a convenient substitute. Sprinkle them on top of any soup. Thick purees like squash, lentil, or split pea are especially good with cereal croutons on top. Or try one of the following:

Pasta with Cereal Crumbs: Instead of using bread crumbs in this classic Italian dish, toss your spaghetti with extra-virgin olive oil and the cereal of your choice sautéed in butter and seasoned with minced garlic, salt, and abundant ground black pepper.

Shrimp with Cereal Crumbs: Top large peeled and deveined shrimp with a mixture of well-buttered, seasoned cereal crumbs and chopped parsley. Bake in a 450°F oven until the shrimp are pink and cooked through, 10 to 15 minutes. Serve with lemon wedges on the side.

Steamed Cauliflower with Cereal Crumbs: Toss cauliflower (or any other steamed vegetable—broccoli, asparagus, and green beans are all good) with buttered cereal crumbs and chopped fresh sage.

Mussels or Clams Oreganato: Place each steamed mussel or clam in a half shell and top with a mixture of buttered cereal crumbs, minced garlic, parlsey, chopped fresh oregano, salt, and ground black pepper. Arrange the mussels or clams on a baking sheet and broil for a minute or two until the topping is crispy and browned.

# grape-nuts tabbouleh

Tabbouleh is a traditional Middle Eastern salad made with cracked wheat (otherwise known as bulgur). Grape-Nuts cereal is a handy no-cook substitution, giving the dish the same whole-grain wheatiness and a little more crunch. Thirty minutes is just the right amount of time to soften up the cereal without letting it get soggy. If you'd like, you can stir together all of the ingredients except the cereal up to 3 hours ahead of time, and then stir in the Grape-Nuts a half hour before you want to eat the salad. Serve with hearts of Romaine lettuce, and use the leaves to scoop up the tabbouleh.

1 cup Grape-Nuts

1 pint cherry tomatoes, quartered

4 scallions, white and light green parts only, finely chopped

1 cup fresh parsley, finely chopped

½ cup fresh mint leaves, finely chopped

¼ cup extra-virgin olive oil

¼ cup freshly squeezed lemon juice

¼ teaspoon allspice

Salt

Freshly ground black pepper

1. In a medium bowl, combine the Grape-Nuts, tomatoes, scallions, parsley, and mint.
2. Whisk together the olive oil, lemon juice, and allspice in a small bowl.
3. Pour the dressing over the Grape-Nuts mixture and stir to combine. Season with salt and pepper to taste. Let stand at room temperature for 30 minutes, stirring once or twice, before serving.

## What Are Grape-Nuts?

If you're not a regular consumer of this versatile cereal that came on the market in 1897, you may not know that it is made from neither grapes nor nuts. Grape-Nuts are crunchy little pellets of wheat and barley. They were so named because cereal magnate C. W. Post mistakenly believed that the maltose sugar originally used to sweeten the cereal was extracted from grapes. He added "nuts" because of the nutty flavor of the grains.

# corn and potato chowder
# with crisped bacon and cornflake topping

This quick soup has a wonderful mix of flavors and textures. If fresh corn is out of season, frozen corn kernels will work just fine.

¼ pound bacon, cut into ½-inch pieces

1 cup cornflakes

1 small onion, finely chopped

2 medium Yukon gold potatoes (about 10 ounces)

2 cups chicken stock or low-sodium canned broth

1 tablespoon all-purpose flour

2 cups buttermilk

2 ½ cups whole corn kernels

Salt

1. In a 3-quart saucepan, cook the bacon until crisp. Add the cornflakes to the pot and stir to combine. Transfer the bacon and cornflake mixture to a paper towel–lined plate with a slotted spoon and set aside. Leave I tablespoon bacon fat in the saucepan and discard the rest.

2. Add the onion to the saucepan and cook over medium heat until softened and translucent, about 5 minutes. Add the potatoes and chicken stock and bring to a boil. Lower the heat, cover, and simmer for 10 minutes.

3. In a small bowl, whisk together the flour and ¼ cup of the buttermilk. Add the remaining 1¾ cups buttermilk and the corn to the saucepan. Stir in the flour mixture. Simmer until the potatoes are very soft but still holding their shape, about 10 minutes. Season with salt to taste.

4. Ladle the soup into bowls and sprinkle some of the bacon and cornflake mixture over each portion. Serve immediately.

# classic macaroni and cheese

If you love crisp topping just as much as the creamy macaroni, you will love this version of the classic, heavily coated with buttery-crisp cornflakes.

**TOPPING**

1 1/2 cups cornflakes, lightly crushed

1 1/2 tablespoons unsalted butter, melted

1/4 teaspoon salt

1/4 teaspoon paprika

**MACARONI**

2 large eggs

One 12-ounce can evaporated milk

1/4 teaspoon Tabasco sauce

1/2 teaspoon dry mustard

3/4 pound elbow macaroni

1 teaspoon salt, or more to taste

1/4 cup (1/2 stick) unsalted butter

12 ounces sharp Cheddar cheese, grated
  (about 3 cups)

1. Make the Topping: In a medium bowl, combine the cornflakes, melted butter, salt, and paprika and set aside.

2. Make the Macaroni: In a small bowl, whisk together the eggs, 1 cup of the evaporated milk, the Tabasco, and mustard in a small bowl and set aside.

3. Bring a large saucepan of water to boil. Add the macaroni and salt. Cook until almost tender (you want the macaroni to be a minute or two from being fully cooked so that it doesn't get mushy when cooked again). Drain, return to the pot, and toss with the butter over low heat until melted.

4. Add the egg mixture and about three-quarters of the cheese to the macaroni and stir until the cheese is melted. Constantly stirring, slowly add the remaining evaporated milk and the remaining cheese. Continue to stir until creamy and piping hot, about 5 minutes. Season with salt if necessary.

5. Transfer the mixture to a broiler-safe 8-inch-square baking pan and sprinkle with the cornflakes. Broil until the cornflakes are deep golden, 1 to 2 minutes. Watch carefully because the cornflakes will burn very soon after they brown.

6. Let cool for 2 minutes and serve immediately.

# potato and ham gratin
# with wheat and bran topping

The wheat and bran cereal topping cuts the richness of this delicious gratin. If you'd like, you can assemble it and refrigerate until ready to bake. A refrigerated gratin will take an extra 5 to 10 minutes in the oven to heat through.

2 tablespoons unsalted butter, melted, plus more
   for greasing the dish

2 pounds russet potatoes, peeled

Salt

2 ounces (about 1/2 cup) diced cooked ham

1 1/4 cups (3 1/2 ounces) grated Gruyère cheese

2 teaspoons finely chopped fresh sage

Freshly ground black pepper

1 medium clove garlic

1/2 cup All-Bran

1/2 cup Wheaties

1. Preheat the oven to 350°F. Butter a 9-inch-round gratin dish.

2. Place the potatoes in a pot and cover with water. Add 1 teaspoon salt and bring to a boil. Boil until the potatoes are partially cooked but still a little hard at the center, about 8 minutes. Drain and set aside to cool slightly. Cut into 1/4-inch-thick rounds.

3. In a small bowl, toss the ham, 1 cup of the Gruyère, and the sage. Arrange half of the potato rounds, overlapping them slightly, in concentric circles in the prepared dish. Season with a little salt and pepper. Sprinkle with the ham and cheese mixture. Arrange the remaining potato rounds on top in concentric circles. Season with salt and pepper.

4. Melt the 2 tablespoons of butter in a heavy saucepan. Add the garlic and cook, turning the clove occasionally, until it is browned on all sides, about 4 minutes. Remove and discard. Add both cereals and 1/4 teaspoon salt and cook, stirring, until the cereal has absorbed the butter, 1 to 2 minutes. Remove from the heat and stir in the remaining 1/4 cup of Gruyère. Sprinkle the cereal mixture over the potatoes. Cover with foil.

5. Bake the gratin until it is heated through, about 30 minutes. Uncover and bake until the topping crisps, about 5 minutes longer. Let stand for 10 minutes and serve warm.

# crispy baked sweet potatoes

Sweet potatoes are always better with a little butter and brown sugar. Here, they're a lot better, with some Grape-Nuts added to the mix.

4 small sweet potatoes (about 2 pounds), peeled
    and halved lengthwise

3 tablespoons melted unsalted butter

¼ teaspoon salt

¾ cup Grape-Nuts

1 ½ tablespoons Dijon mustard

1 tablespoon light brown sugar

1. Preheat the oven to 350°F. Line a baking sheet with aluminum foil.
2. Make cuts in the rounded sides of the potatoes, about 1 inch apart, cutting almost, but not all the way, through the potatoes. Brush with about 1 tablespoon of the butter and sprinkle with salt. Bake, flat side down, until soft, 30 to 35 minutes.
3. While the potatoes are baking, in a small bowl, combine the Grape-Nuts, mustard, brown sugar, and remaining butter. Turn the potatoes over so they are flat side up. Sprinkle the potatoes with the cereal mixture. Return the potatoes to the oven and bake until the topping is golden, 10 minutes more. Serve immediately.

# pappa al pomodoro, american style

Tuscan cooks make amazing soup from nothing more than tomatoes, olive oil, and garlic, with stale bread stirred in for bulk and texture. Why shouldn't American cooks use leftover cereal to conjure a version of our own? Here I use Wheaties, but other unsweetened cereals, such as cornflakes or crispy rice cereal, would work just as well.

¼ cup extra-virgin olive oil

2 medium cloves garlic, finely chopped

Two 14 ½-ounce cans diced tomatoes, drained

8 large fresh basil leaves, cut into thin strips

Salt

Freshly ground black pepper

2 cups chicken stock or low-sodium canned broth

2 cups water

2 cups Wheaties

1. In a medium pot or soup kettle, heat the oil. Add the garlic and cook, stirring, over medium heat until golden, about 2 minutes. Add the tomatoes and cook until softened, about 10 minutes.

2. Season the tomatoes with salt and pepper to taste. Add the stock and water and bring to a boil. Lower the heat and simmer until the flavors are combined, about 5 minutes.

3. Stir in the cereal and simmer until it absorbs some of the liquid, about 2 minutes. Cover the pot and remove from the heat. Let stand until the cereal softens and breaks down, about 15 minutes. Adjust the seasonings, rewarm, and serve immediately.

# main dishes

Whether used as a filler in meat loaf (Old-Fashioned Meat Loaf with Wheaties), meatballs (Middle Eastern Lamb Meatballs in Pita Breads with Minted Yogurt Sauce), or burgers (Turkey Burgers with Year-Round Tomato Salsa), as a crunchy coating for fish fillets (Cap'n Crunch–Crusted Fish Fillets with Chipotle Tartar Sauce), or as a thickener for chili (Turkey and Red Bean Chili), cereal is a great starting point for many quick, tasty, and nutritious weeknight dinners.

# italian-style meat loaf
# with semolina and spinach

This delicious meat loaf has spinach, smoked mozzarella cheese, and semolina, otherwise known as Cream of Wheat®. Make sure to squeeze out all the excess water from the spinach after it is thawed, so your meat loaf is moist but not watery. For a complete meal, serve with a green salad dressed with oil and vinegar, and pasta shells with tomato sauce.

2 pounds ground round

1 large yellow onion, finely chopped

2 cloves garlic, finely chopped

1 large egg

½ cup Cream of Wheat, uncooked

½ cup tomato paste

1 cup (3 ½ ounces) grated smoked mozzarella cheese

One 10-ounce package frozen chopped spinach, thawed, excess water squeezed out

1 teaspoon salt, or to taste

Freshly ground black pepper

1. Preheat the oven to 350°F. Line a rimmed baking sheet with heavy-duty aluminum foil.

2. In a large bowl, combine the ground round, onion, garlic, egg, Cream of Wheat, tomato paste, mozzarella cheese, spinach, salt, and pepper and mix with a fork or your hands until evenly blended.

3. With wet hands, pat the mixture into a loaf shape approximately 9×5 inches. Place on the foil-lined rimmed baking sheet.

4. Bake the loaf until the exterior is crisp and the meat is cooked through (160°F on an instant-read thermometer), about 1 hour. Let stand for 15 minutes before slicing and serving warm.

# middle eastern lamb meatballs
# in pita breads with minted yogurt sauce

These exotically spiced meatballs can also be wrapped in warm flour tortillas, or served on their own as hors d'oeuvres.

2 teaspoons olive oil

1 small onion, finely chopped

2 garlic cloves, finely chopped

1 pound ground lamb

1 cup crispy rice cereal, lightly crushed

1 large egg

½ cup finely chopped fresh cilantro

1 teaspoon salt

¼ teaspoon cayenne

¼ teaspoon allspice

Pinch cinnamon

1 cup plain yogurt

½ small cucumber, peeled, seeded, and
   chopped

2 tablespoons finely chopped fresh mint leaves

4 pita breads

1. Preheat the oven to 450°F. Set a wire rack above a baking dish. Pour about ¼ inch of water into the dish.

2. Heat the olive oil in a small skillet over medium heat. Cook the onion, stirring, until softened, about 5 minutes. Add the garlic and cook, stirring, until fragrant, about 1 minute more. Scrape into a large mixing bowl and let cool.

3. Add the lamb, cereal, egg, cilantro, salt, cayenne, allspice, and cinnamon to the bowl and stir until all the ingredients are well combined.

4. Scoop level tablespoons of the lamb mixture and roll them into balls between the palms of your hands. Set the shaped meatballs on the rack, an inch apart from one another. Bake until lightly browned and just cooked through, 15 to 20 minutes.

5. While the meatballs are cooking, mix together the yogurt, cucumber, and mint. Serve the warm meatballs inside the pita breads with the yogurt sauce on the side.

# old-fashioned meat loaf with wheaties

This meat loaf comes courtesy of my friend Cheryl Merser. It is adapted from a recipe in her fun and supremely helpful book, *Relax! It's Only Dinner*. Using crushed Wheaties cereal instead of bread crumbs in meat loaf gives this weeknight dinner staple a wonderfully light texture. I think that barbecue sauce makes a more savory meat loaf, but you may substitute ketchup if you prefer. Don't forget to cover your baking sheet with aluminum foil for easy cleanup.

2 pounds ground round

1 large yellow onion, finely chopped

1 large egg

1 ¼ cups Wheaties or cornflakes

½ cup barbecue sauce

1 cup (3 ½ ounces) grated Cheddar cheese

1 teaspoon salt, or to taste

Freshly ground black pepper

4 strips bacon

1. Preheat the oven to 350°F. Line a rimmed baking sheet with heavy-duty aluminum foil.
2. In a large bowl, combine the ground round, onion, egg, cereal, barbecue sauce, cheese, salt, and pepper, and mix with a fork or your hands until evenly blended.
3. With wet hands, pat the mixture into a loaf shape approximately 9×5 inches. Place on the foil-lined rimmed baking sheet. Lay the bacon strips on top of the meat loaf in 2 crisscrosses.
4. Bake the loaf until the bacon is crisp and the meat is cooked through (160°F on an instant-read thermometer), about 1 hour. Let stand for 15 minutes before slicing and serving warm.

# whole wheat pizza
# with arugula and bacon

You can top this pizza dough with anything you like, but the slightly bitter greens with a sprinkling of smoky, salty bacon really stand up to the hearty flavor and texture of the bran. The recipe makes enough dough for 2 pizzas. Freeze half the dough and save it for another night.

## DOUGH

1 ¾ cups warm water

1 envelope (2 ½ teaspoons) rapid-rise yeast

3 cups all-purpose flour

1 cup All-Bran

1 ½ teaspoons salt

2 tablespoons olive oil

## TOPPING

6 ounces (6 or 7 slices) bacon, cut into
    1-inch strips

3 cups loosely packed arugula, washed
    and dried

1 tablespoon olive oil

Salt

Freshly ground black pepper

1 ½ cups (6 ounces) grated mozzarella cheese

½ cup freshly grated parmesan cheese

1. Make the Dough: Measure the warm water into a glass measuring cup and whisk in the yeast. Let the mixture stand for 5 minutes to give the yeast a chance to dissolve.

2. Place the flour, cereal, and salt in a food processor and pulse 2 or 3 times to combine. With the motor running, pour the yeast mixture and olive oil into the feed tube and process until the dough forms a smooth ball. To knead, continue to process for 30 seconds. Coat the inside of a large mixing bowl with cooking spray. Shape the dough into a rough ball and place it in the bowl. Cover the bowl with

(continued on page 66)

plastic wrap and let the dough stand in a warm, draft-free spot until it has doubled in size, I to I ½ hours.

3. Preheat the oven to 500°F.

4. Punch down the dough and cut it in half with a sharp chef's knife. Place one half in a bowl, cover with plastic wrap, and let rest for 20 minutes. (Place the other half in an airtight container and freeze for up to two months. Defrost the dough on the counter for 5 or 6 hours before using.)

5. While the dough is resting, make the Topping: In a skillet over medium heat, cook the bacon until it is browned and most of the fat is rendered, about 6 minutes. Drain on paper towels. In a large bowl, combine the arugula, bacon, olive oil, and salt and pepper to taste in a large bowl.

6. Turn the pizza dough out onto a lightly floured baking sheet and press it into a 14-inch circle. Spoon the arugula mixture over the pizza, leaving a I-inch border of dough. Sprinkle with the grated mozzarella cheese.

7. Bake the pizza until the edges of the crust are well browned and the cheese is golden and bubbling, I2 to I5 minutes. Sprinkle the parmesan cheese over the pizza and continue to bake until the parmesan is melted, an additional I to 2 minutes. Remove the pizza from the oven and serve immediately.

# cap'n crunch–crusted fish fillets with chipotle tartar sauce

SERVES 4

These fish fillets are topped with a sprinkling of sweet, cornbreadlike crumbs made from Cap'n Crunch cereal. Smokey, spicy tartar sauce provides great contrast. Canned chipotle chiles are available in most supermarkets and Latin grocery stores. Seeded and chopped fresh jalapeños may be substituted if you like.

$\frac{1}{2}$ cup mayonnaise

$\frac{1}{4}$ cup plain yogurt

2 tablespoons finely chopped dill pickle

2 teaspoons finely chopped chipotle chiles in adobo sauce

1 small clove garlic, finely chopped

2 teaspoons finely chopped cilantro

1 teaspoon fresh lime juice

$\frac{3}{4}$ cup Cap'n Crunch, crushed

$\frac{1}{4}$ cup unseasoned bread crumbs

2 tablespoons unsalted butter, melted and cooled

$\frac{1}{2}$ teaspoon salt

1 pound flounder fillets

1. To make the tartar sauce, in a small bowl, combine the mayonnaise, yogurt, pickle, chiles, garlic, cilantro, and lime juice and stir. Cover with plastic wrap and refrigerate until ready to serve.

2. Preheat the oven to 450°F. Cover a rimmed baking sheet with heavy-duty aluminum foil.

3. In a small bowl, combine the cereal crumbs, bread crumbs, 1 tablespoon of the melted butter, and $\frac{1}{4}$ teaspoon of the salt and set aside.

4. Place the flounder fillets on the baking sheet. Brush with the remaining tablespoon of butter and sprinkle with the remaining $\frac{1}{4}$ teaspoon salt. Bake until the fillets turn white, about 6 minutes. Remove from the oven and turn the broiler to high. Spread the cereal mixture on top of the fish and broil just until the crumbs start to color, 30 seconds to 1 minute. Remove from the oven and serve immediately with the tartar sauce on the side.

## Cap'n Crunch: AN APPRECIATION

This cereal classic remains as popular today as it was when it debuted in 1963 with the slogan "Stays crunchy, even in milk." Cap'n Crunch was the first breakfast cereal to link itself to a cartoon character and market itself directly to children who watched Saturday morning cartoons. Children's advocates often point the finger at Cap'n Crunch as the initiator of the ceaseless stream of ads aimed at kids. But if you are of a certain age, you can't help feeling affection for Cap'n Crunch, even as you stroll the cereal aisle with your children hanging from the shopping cart, begging and screaming for the Trix® Rabbit and Count Chocula®.

Cap'n Crunch was dreamed up by cartoonists working for Jay Ward, the creator of Rocky and Bullwinkle and George of the Jungle. The Ward studio's signature silliness was evident in commercials featuring the Cap'n, his crew of four kids, his dog, and his nemesis, pirate Jean LaFoot, who was always trying, and failing, to steal the cereal ("You can't get away with the Crunch, because the Crunch always gives you away!"). Surveys in the late '60s showed that Cap'n Crunch was the most recognized cartoon character on TV. Although he's been joined by a platoon of cartoon pitchmen since, he is the most enduring. While other characters have come and gone (anyone remember King Vitaman?), he is still sailing the seas with his store of crunchy little corn barrels.

It had been years since I tasted my favorite sweetened breakfast cereal, and when I had my first bite I was pleasantly surprised at the delightful corn flavor as well as the crunch. Although I no longer eat it for breakfast, I love to cook with Cap'n Crunch because it lends flavor and crunch to dishes as disparate as fish fillets and cheesecake crust.

# cap'n crunch and salmon croquettes

Maybe it's because of the "Cap'n," but Cap'n Crunch truly does wonders for seafood. Here, it's used as a binder for salmon cakes, its sweetness balancing the salty, strong flavor of the salmon. If you'd like, you may substitute fresh salmon for the canned in this recipe. Just remove all skin and bones and cut into ¼-inch dice before proceeding.

Two 7 ½-ounce cans salmon, drained and flaked

1 cup Cap'n Crunch, crushed

¾ cup mayonnaise

2 scallions, white and light green parts only, finely chopped

1 ½ tablespoons fresh lemon juice

2 teaspoons dried thyme

¼ teaspoon salt

1 large egg

1 tablespoon horseradish

2 tablespoons unsalted butter

Lemon wedges, for serving

1. In a medium bowl, combine the salmon, crushed cereal, ¼ cup of the mayonnaise, I tablespoon of the lemon juice, I ½ teaspoons of the thyme, salt, scallions, and egg and stir gently to blend. Shape the mixture into 8 patties, about ¾ inch thick. Place them on a plate and place in the freezer for 20 minutes to firm up.

2. In a small bowl, combine the remaining ½ cup mayonnaise, ½ tablespoon lemon juice, and ½ teaspoon thyme, and the horseradish. Refrigerate until ready to serve.

3. Heat the butter in a large skillet over medium-low heat. Add the salmon croquettes and cook until browned and heated through, about 5 minutes on each side. Serve with the mayonnaise and lemon wedges on the side.

# mustard-dill salmon fillets
# with a crispy cornflake crust

This is one of the simplest and most reliable ways to cook salmon so that it is tender and pink on the inside with a delectable outside crunch. Cornflakes are the key ingredient in the topping. They toast beautifully under the broiler. Just watch them carefully—seconds after they are perfectly browned, they will begin to smoke and burn.

1 ½ cup cornflakes, crushed

2 tablespoons finely chopped fresh dill

¾ teaspoons salt

4 salmon fillets, each weighing 6 to 7 ounces

1 teaspoon vegetable oil

Freshly ground black pepper

1 ½ tablespoons Dijon mustard

1. Place an oven rack in the top position of your oven, closest to the broiler. Place a second rack in the position immediately below that one. Preheat the broiler. Cover a rimmed baking sheet with heavy-duty aluminum foil.

2. In a small bowl, combine the cereal, dill, and ¼ teaspoon of the salt.

3. Place the salmon fillets on the baking sheet. Brush them with the oil and sprinkle with the remaining ½ teaspoon salt and the pepper. Broil the salmon on the upper rack until the surface is beginning to brown and the outer edges of the fillets are opaque, 8 to 10 minutes.

4. Remove the pan from the oven and spread the mustard over the fish. Press the cereal mixture onto the fillets, pressing lightly on it with the back of a spoon so it adheres to the fish.

5. Return the pan to the lower rack of the oven and continue to broil until the crust is deep golden, about 30 seconds. Watch the fish carefully because the crust will burn quickly as soon as it has browned. Remove from the oven, and use a large spatula to remove each fillet to a dinner plate. Serve immediately.

# oven-crisped chicken breasts

This is a fantastic alternative to fried chicken, with just as much crispy appeal but a lot less mess. The cornflakes give the coating crunch. The mayonnaise helps the coating adhere and keeps the chicken moist as it bakes. Try it once and you may retire your frying pan.

4 cups cornflakes

1 teaspoon salt, or more to taste

¾ teaspoon garlic powder

½ teaspoon dried rosemary, finely chopped

6 tablespoons mayonnaise

4 boneless, skinless chicken breasts, about 1 ½ pounds, trimmed of fat and tendons, rinsed, and patted dry

1. Preheat the oven to 425°F. Set a wire rack on top of a rimmed baking sheet.
2. Combine the cornflakes, salt, garlic powder, and rosemary in a zipper-lock plastic bag and crush with a rolling pin. Transfer the crumbs to a large bowl and stir in 2 tablespoons of the mayonnaise until the crumbs are sticky and clumping together.
3. Coat the chicken on both sides with the remaining 4 tablespoons mayonnaise. Press the underside of each chicken breast into the crumb mixture so that the crumbs adhere, and transfer the breasts to the rack, crumbed side down. Press an even coating of the remaining crumbs on the tops of the breasts.
4. Bake until the coating is crispy and the chicken is cooked through, 25 to 30 minutes (160°F on an instant-read thermometer). Serve immediately.

# crisp turkey cutlets
# with cranberry pan sauce

Cereal coatings on thicker cuts of meat will burn in a sauté pan before the meat is cooked, but the coating will crisp to perfection on thin turkey cutlets. A quick pan sauce of dried cranberries is a simple and colorful accompaniment.

½ cup dried cranberries

¼ cup all-purpose flour

1 large egg

1 tablespoon water

1 ½ cups Wheaties or other whole wheat
   cereal flakes, finely crushed

6 turkey cutlets (about 1 ½ pounds), rinsed
   and patted dry

Salt

Freshly ground black pepper

4 tablespoons (½ stick) unsalted butter

2 tablespoons olive oil

2 shallots, finely chopped

1 clove garlic, finely chopped

1 cup chicken stock or low-sodium canned
   chicken broth

¼ cup finely chopped fresh chives

1. Place the cranberries in a heatproof bowl and cover with boiling water. Soak until softened, about 15 minutes. Drain and set aside.

2. Place the flour in a shallow bowl or pie plate. Lightly beat the egg and water in another shallow bowl or pie plate. Place the crushed cereal in another shallow bowl or pie plate.

3. Sprinkle the cutlets with salt and pepper. Working with 1 cutlet at a time, dredge both sides in flour and shake over the bowl to remove any excess. Next, dip the cutlet in the egg to coat, letting any excess drip back into the bowl. Press first one side of the cutlet and then the other in the cereal to coat lightly but completely. Repeat with the remaining cutlets.

4. Heat 1 tablespoon of the butter and 1 tablespoon of the oil in a large, heavy, non-

*(continued on page 78)*

stick skillet over medium-high heat. When the foaming has subsided, lay half of the cutlets in the skillet and cook until browned on one side, about 2 minutes. Turn and cook on the other side until both sides are well browned and the meat feels firm when pressed, 1 to 2 minutes longer. Transfer the cutlets to a warmed serving platter, add another tablespoon of butter and another tablespoon of oil to the pan, and repeat with the remaining cutlets.

5. Turn the heat down to medium and add the shallots to the empty skillet. Cook, stirring, until softened, 3 to 4 minutes. Add the garlic and cook, stirring, for another minute. Add the chicken stock and cranberries and bring to a boil, stirring with a wooden spoon to loosen any browned bits from the bottom of the pan. Simmer until the mixture is thickened, 2 to 3 minutes. Remove the pan from the heat and swirl in the remaining 2 tablespoons butter and the chives. Pour the sauce over the cooked cutlets and serve immediately.

# turkey burgers with year-round tomato salsa

Special K cereal binds the ground turkey, and yogurt keeps the burgers moist in this superfast, nutritious recipe. You can just serve burgers with ketchup, but the salsa ensures that they will be juicy. For safe eating, turkey should be cooked to an internal temperature of 160°F. Insert an instant-read thermometer into the center of the meat for an accurate reading.

**SALSA**

One 14-ounce can diced tomatoes, drained

1 small jalapeño chile, or to taste, seeded and minced

1 clove garlic, finely chopped

2 tablespoons finely chopped fresh cilantro

¼ teaspoon salt

1 teaspoon fresh lime juice

**BURGERS**

1 cup Special K, crushed

¼ cup plain yogurt

1 tablespoon Worcestershire sauce

½ teaspoon salt

1 clove garlic, finely chopped

1 ¼ pounds lean ground turkey

1 large egg

1 tablespoon vegetable oil

4 hamburger buns

1. Make the Salsa: In a small bowl, combine the tomatoes, chile, garlic, cilantro, salt, and lime juice. Cover and let stand at room temperature to allow the flavors to meld until ready to serve.

2. Make the Burgers: In a medium bowl, combine the cereal, yogurt, Worcestershire sauce, salt, and garlic and let stand until the cereal softens, about 5 minutes.

3. Add the turkey and egg and gently mix until the ingredients are well combined. Shape the mixture into four ¾-inch-thick patties.

*(continued on page 80)*

4. Heat the oil in a large nonstick skillet over medium heat. Add the burgers and cook without moving until the bottom of each one has a dark brown crust, 3 to 4 minutes. Carefully flip the burgers (they will be softer than burgers made from ground beef), and continue to cook for another 3 minutes. Turn the heat to low and cook until the burgers are cooked through and the center registers 160°F on an instant-read thermometer, another 2 to 4 minutes. Remove from the heat and serve immediately on buns, passing the salsa on the side.

# turkey and red bean chili

Traditional chili recipes are thickened with cornstarch or masa harina, but All-Bran cereal thickens this lighter chili and adds some wholesome fiber to the dish. Lean ground turkey makes this dish especially healthful (you may substitute ground chicken or extra-lean ground sirloin if you like). Serve with bowls of chopped white onion, avocado, cilantro, or reduced-fat Jack cheese on the side.

2 tablespoons vegetable or canola oil

2 pounds ground turkey

Salt

2 cups finely chopped onion

2 cloves garlic, finely chopped

3 tablespoons chili powder, or more to taste

1 teaspoon ground cumin

Cayenne

2 cups canned crushed tomatoes

3 cups water

½ cup All-Bran, finely crushed in a
   blender or food processor

Two 15-ounce cans red kidney beans, drained
   and rinsed

1. Heat 1 tablespoon of the oil in a large, heavy soup kettle or Dutch oven over medium-high heat. Add the turkey and 1½ teaspoons salt and cook, stirring frequently, until the meat loses its raw color, 10 to 12 minutes. Transfer the cooked turkey and cooking juices to a bowl and set aside.

2. Add the remaining tablespoon of oil to the pan, turn the heat down to medium, and add the onion. Cook, stirring frequently, until the onion becomes translucent, about 5 minutes. Add the garlic and cook, stirring, for an additional minute. Stir in the chili powder, cumin, and cayenne pepper to taste and cook, stirring, for 1 more minute.

3. Return the turkey to the pot and stir in the tomatoes and 3 cups of the water. Bring to a simmer, cover, and cook at a bare simmer for 2 hours.

4. Stir the cereal into the chili and simmer until the juices are thickened, about 5 minutes. Stir in the beans, season with additional salt if necessary, and cook until the beans are heated through, another 5 minutes.

# sweet treats and desserts

Cereal can be transformed into a sweet for any occasion. Try Tropical Fruit and Cereal Clusters held together with white chocolate as an afternoon energy pick-me-up; Cocoa Krispies Peanut Butter Brownies for the lunchbox, Apple Crisp with Cheerios and Almond Topping served warm at Sunday dinner, or Frosted Flakes Shortcakes with Peaches and Cream for company at a summer barbecue.

# tropical fruit and cereal clusters

Any time I can work tropical fruit, nuts, and white chocolate into a single recipe, I will, since this is one of my all-time favorite combinations. The spoon-size shredded wheat prevents these delectable mouthfuls from being too sweet. Sunsweet makes a tropical fruit mix, but you can always mix your own combination, or choose a single favorite fruit of your choice. Pineapple and mango are both great.

1 cup spoon-size shredded wheat

1 1/3 cups (6 ounces) tropical dried fruit mix or
   1 1/3 cups dried pineapple or mango,
   coarsely chopped

6 ounces white chocolate, finely
   chopped

1/2 cup salted cashews or macadamia nuts

1. Line a baking sheet with parchment or wax paper.

2. In a medium bowl, combine the cereal, nuts, and dried fruit.

3. Put 1 inch of water in the bottom of a double boiler or a large saucepan and bring to a bare simmer. Place the white chocolate in the top of the double boiler or in a stainless-steel bowl big enough to rest on top of the saucepan, and set it on top of the simmering water, making sure that the water doesn't touch the bottom of the bowl. Heat, whisking occasionally, until the chocolate is completely melted. Remove from heat and whisk until completely smooth. Stir it into the cereal mixture.

4. Spoon tablespoonfuls onto the prepared baking sheet. Place the baking sheet in the refrigerator until the chocolate has hardened, about 1/2 hour. This will keep at room temperature in an airtight container for up to 1 week.

## Who Invented Shredded Wheat?

The Kellogg brothers were not the only turn-of-the-century inventors slow to see the commercial possibilities of cereal. Shredded wheat was a similarly accidental success.

Henry Perky and William H. Ford developed the recipe for shredded wheat to demonstrate their biscuit-making machine to potential customers. People weren't interested in the machine but liked the cereal. Perky established the bakery that was to grow into Nabisco and started mass-manufacturing shredded wheat only after his machine failed to catch on with bakers.

# milk chocolate and cherry crunch

Bittersweet or semisweet chocolate may be substituted for the milk chocolate, and raisins or dried cranberries may be substituted for the cherries in this simple candy that's perfect for munching while watching a movie.

1 cup (one 6-ounce bag) milk chocolate chips
   or 6 ounces milk chocolate, chopped
1 tablespoon unsalted butter

1 cup Cocoa Krispies
½ cup dried cherries

1. Line an 8-inch-square baking pan with heavy-duty aluminum foil, making sure that the foil is tucked into all the corners and that there is at least 1 inch overhanging the top of the pan on all sides.

2. Put 1 inch of water in the bottom of a double boiler or a large saucepan and bring to a bare simmer. Place the chocolate chips and butter in the top of the double boiler or in a stainless-steel bowl big enough to rest on top of the saucepan, and set it on top of the simmering water, making sure that the water doesn't touch the bottom of the bowl. Heat, whisking occasionally, until the chocolate and butter are completely melted. Remove from heat and whisk until completely smooth. Stir in the Cocoa Krispies and cherries.

3. Spread the chocolate mixture across the bottom of the foil-covered baking pan in an even layer with a spatula. Refrigerate until hardened, about 1 hour. Break into pieces. This will keep in an airtight container in the refrigerator for up to 3 days.

# crispy chocolate chip cookies

Crispy rice cereal gives these cookies incredible lightness and crunch. This is a great recipe to turn to when you want a crunchy cookie but don't want to use nuts.

1 ¼ cups unbleached all-purpose flour

½ teaspoon baking soda

½ teaspoon salt

½ cup (1 stick) unsalted butter, melted and cooled slightly

½ cup firmly packed light brown sugar

½ cup granulated sugar

1 large egg

1 teaspoon vanilla extract

1 cup semisweet chocolate chips

2 cups crispy rice cereal

1. Preheat the oven to 350°F.
2. In a medium bowl, combine the flour, baking soda, and salt.
3. In a large mixing bowl with a wooden spoon, cream together the melted butter and both sugars until smooth. Add the egg and vanilla and beat until smooth. Stir in the flour mixture until just incorporated. Stir in the chocolate chips and cereal. Place the bowl in the refrigerator for 10 minutes (or for up to 6 hours) to let the dough firm up.
4. Drop the batter by heaping tablespoonfuls onto ungreased baking sheets, leaving about 3 inches between each cookie. (Balls of dough may be placed next to one another on parchment-lined baking sheets, frozen, transferred to zipper-lock plastic freezer bags, and stored in the freezer for up to 1 month. Frozen cookies may be placed in the oven directly from the freezer and baked as directed.)
5. Bake the cookies until golden around the edges but still soft on top, 10 to 12 minutes (a minute or two longer for frozen dough). Let the cookies stand on the baking sheet for 5 minutes, and then remove them with a metal spatula to a wire rack to cool completely. The cookies will keep in an airtight container for 2 to 3 days.

# secret ingredient oatmeal-chip cookies

You may not be able to detect the Special K cereal in these cookies, but that is what is giving them their wonderful texture and flavor.

1 cup unbleached all-purpose flour

1/2 teaspoon baking soda

1/4 teaspoon baking powder

1/4 teaspoon salt

1/2 cup (1 stick) unsalted butter, melted and cooled

1/2 cup granulated sugar

1/2 cup firmly packed light brown sugar

1 large egg

1 teaspoon vanilla extract

1 cup old-fashioned (not quick-cooking) oats

1 cup Special K

1 cup semisweet or milk chocolate chips

1/2 cup sweetened flaked coconut

1. Preheat the oven to 350°F.

2. In a medium bowl, combine the flour, baking soda, baking powder, and salt.

3. In a large mixing bowl with a wooden spoon, cream together the melted butter and both sugars until smooth. Add the egg and vanilla and beat until smooth. Stir in the flour mixture until just incorporated. Stir in the oats and Special K. Stir in the chocolate chips and coconut. Place the bowl in the refrigerator for 10 minutes (or for up to 6 hours) to let the dough firm up.

4. Drop the batter by heaping tablespoonfuls onto ungreased baking sheets, leaving about 3 inches between each cookie. (Balls of dough may be placed next to one another on parchment-lined baking sheets, frozen, transferred to zipper-lock plastic freezer bags, and stored in the freezer for up to 1 month. Frozen cookies may be placed in the oven directly from the freezer and baked as directed.)

5. Bake the cookies until golden around the edges but still soft on top, 10 to 12 minutes (a minute or two longer for frozen dough). Let the cookies stand on the baking sheet for 5 minutes, and then remove them with a metal spatula to a wire rack to cool completely. The cookies will keep in an airtight container for 2 to 3 days.

# cocoa krispies peanut butter brownies

Ground Cocoa Krispies in place of flour gives these brownies a deliciously chewy, candylike texture.

2 cups Cocoa Krispies, finely crushed in
a food processor or blender

1/4 teaspoon baking powder

1/4 teaspoon salt

1/2 cup coarsely chopped walnuts

2 ounces unsweetened chocolate, finely chopped

4 tablespoons (1/2 stick) unsalted butter

1 cup sugar

1/4 cup smooth peanut butter

2 large eggs

1. Preheat the oven to 350°F. Line an 8-inch-square baking pan with heavy-duty aluminum foil, making sure that the foil is tucked into all the corners and that there is at least 1 inch overhanging the top of the pan on all sides.

2. In a medium bowl, combine the crushed cereal, baking powder, salt, and nuts.

3. Combine the chocolate and butter in a saucepan and heat over low heat, whisking often, until the chocolate and butter are completely melted. Remove from the heat and stir in the sugar and peanut butter until smooth. Stir in the eggs and stir until smooth. Stir in the cereal mixture.

4. Scrape the batter into the prepared baking pan. Bake until the brownies are just set in the center, 25 to 30 minutes. Let them cool completely in the pan on a wire rack.

5. Grasping the overhanging foil on either side of the pan, lift out the brownies and place on a cutting board. Cut into 16 squares. The brownies will keep at room temperature in an airtight container for up to 3 days.

# crunchy peanut butter ice cream sandwiches

Grape-Nuts make a deliciously crunchy coating for the vanilla ice cream inside these sandwiches. Cornflakes also work very nicely here.

½ cup light corn syrup

½ cup smooth peanut butter

3 cups Grape-Nuts

1 pint vanilla ice cream, slightly softened

1 pint chocolate ice cream, slightly softened

1. Line an 8-inch-square baking pan with heavy-duty aluminum foil, making sure that the foil is tucked into all the corners and that there is at least 1 inch overhanging the top of the pan on all sides.

2. In the bowl of an electric mixer fitted with a whisk attachment, combine the corn syrup and peanut butter. Stir until well combined. Add the cereal and continue to stir with the mixer until all of the cereal is moistened. Spread half of cereal mixture into the bottom of the prepared pan and press it into a thin, even layer with your fingertips. Place in the freezer for 15 minutes.

3. Spoon the vanilla ice cream in tablespoonfuls across the cereal layer. Use a spatula to smooth the ice cream into an even layer. Place in the freezer for 20 minutes to firm up.

4. Smooth the chocolate ice cream over the vanilla ice cream and place in the freezer for another 20 minutes.

5. Spread the remaining cereal mixture over the top of the chocolate ice cream, and press it into a thin, even layer with your fingertips. Freeze until very firm, at least 6 hours and up to 1 day.

6. Grasping the overhanging foil on either side of the pan, lift out the bars and place them on a cutting board. Cut into 8 bars. Serve immediately.

## Simple Cereal and Ice Cream Desserts

If you love cereal, you've probably already discovered that it is a natural partner with ice cream. Here are a few simple ways to combine the two for quick, fun, kid-friendly desserts:

Froot Loops: Roll balls of vanilla ice cream in cereal and freeze on parchment-lined baking sheet until firm. Serve in dishes with hot fudge sauce on top.

Apple Jacks: Same as above, but serve with warm caramel or butterscotch sauce instead.

Honey Smacks: Use instead of nuts when assembling an ice cream sundae or banana split.

Frosted Flakes: Melt 1 tablespoon of butter together with 1½ tablespoons of dark brown sugar and toss with ¼ cup sliced almonds and 1 cup Frosted Flakes. Let cool and use on top of coffee or vanilla ice cream.

Fruity Pebbles: Insert popsicle sticks into peeled bananas, freeze for 1 hour, dip in melted chocolate and then coat with Fruity Pebbles. Return to freezer until chocolate is firm, another 30 minutes.

# apple crisp with cheerios and almond topping

I like this topping with plain Cheerios, but if you have a sweet tooth you may use the apple-cinnamon variety.

3 large tart apples, such as Granny Smith peeled, cored, and cut into 1/2-inch-thick slices

1/3 cup plus 2 tablespoons light brown sugar

1 tablespoon cornstarch

2 cups Cheerios, lightly crushed

1/4 cup sliced almonds

1/8 teaspoon ground cinnamon

Pinch salt

1/4 cup (1/2 stick) unsalted butter, chilled and cut into small pieces

Vanilla ice cream or sweetened whipped cream (optional)

1. Preheat the oven to 375°F.
2. In a medium bowl, combine the apple slices, 1/3 cup of the brown sugar, and the cornstarch in a medium mixing bowl. Let stand, stirring once or twice while preparing the topping, to allow the sugar to dissolve.
3. In a medium bowl, combine the Cheerios, almonds, cinnamon, and salt and stir to combine. Add the butter and mix on low speed with an electric mixer just until clumps begin to form, 1 to 2 minutes.
4. Spread the apples across the bottom of an 8-inch-square baking pan. Scatter the topping over the apples. Bake until the apples are bubbling and the topping is golden, 35 to 40 minutes. Serve warm, with ice cream or whipped cream, if desired.

## A Cereal Kingdom and Its Tiny Subjects

Cheerios were originally called Cheeri-oats and sold starting in 1941 as a ready-to-eat alternative to oatmeal. In the 1950s, General Mills shifted its marketing plan to sell the cereal to parents as a healthy breakfast and snack food for children. Now the brand is the best-selling boxed cereal in the country.

One out of eleven boxes of cereal sold in America is a box of Cheerios (which comes in a range of flavors, including Honey Nut, Frosted, Apple Cinnamon, Multi-Grain, and Berry Burst). Children under the age of 5 consume 23 percent of all Cheerios. Although a lot of them grow up and move on to other brands, enough of them remain loyal to their first finger food to make Cheerios number one.

# strawberry cheesecake with cap'n crunch crust

Here's a great do-ahead dessert when strawberries are in season, a fresh-tasting no-bake cheesecake that couldn't be simpler to make. The crust is deliciously chewy and nutty. Believe it or not, toasting the crushed Cap'n Crunch cereal in the oven really brings out its corn flavor.

CRUST

4 cups Cap'n Crunch (to yield about
    1 1/2 cups crumbs)
1/2 cup pecans or walnuts
5 tablespoons unsalted butter, melted
1/8 teaspoon salt

FILLING

1/4 cup cold water
3 teaspoons unflavored gelatin
12 ounces (1 1/2 packages) cream cheese,
    softened
1 cup heavy cream
1 pint strawberries, washed and hulled
1 cup sugar
1 tablespoon strained fresh lemon juice

1. Preheat the oven to 350°F.

2. Make the Crust: Place the Cap'n Crunch and the nuts in the work bowl of a food processor and process until finely ground. In a medium bowl, combine the crumbs, butter, and salt in a medium-size mixing bowl and stir until the mixture is moistened.

3. Press the mixture evenly across the bottom and about 1 inch up the sides of a 9-inch springform pan, packing it tightly with your fingertips so it is even and compacted. Bake the crust until it is crisp, 6 to 8 minutes. Let cool completely (the crust may be wrapped in plastic and frozen for up to 1 month).

*(continued on page 100)*

4. Make the Filling: Place the cold water in a small bowl and sprinkle the gelatin on top. Let the gelatin stand to dissolve. In the work bowl of a food processor, combine the cream cheese, heavy cream, strawberries, sugar, and lemon juice and process the mixture until it is smooth.

5. Put 1 inch of water in a small saucepan and bring the pot to a bare simmer. Place the bowl containing the gelatin on top of the simmering water and heat, whisking constantly, just until the gelatin melts, 30 seconds to 1 minute. With the food processor running, pour the gelatin mixture through the feed tube into the strawberry mixture and process to create a smooth puree.

6. Scrape the filling into the prepared crust. Cover with plastic wrap and refrigerate it until the filling is completely set, at least 6 hours and up to 1 day.

# creamy espresso pie
# with cocoa krispies crust

To make an even simpler version of this coffee-and-chocolate-lover's icebox pie, substitute 2 pints of coffee ice cream for the cream cheese filling.

CRUST

3 tablespoons light corn syrup

1 tablespoon sugar

1 1/2 tablespoons unsalted butter

2 cups Cocoa Krispies

FILLING

One 8-ounce package cream cheese, softened

One 15-ounce can sweetened condensed milk

1 tablespoon instant espresso powder

1/2 teaspoon vanilla extract

WARM CHOCOLATE SAUCE

8 ounces bittersweet chocolate, finely chopped

1/4 cup water

1 tablespoon coffee liqueur (optional)

1. Make the Crust: Butter a 9-inch pie pan. In a small heavy saucepan, combine the corn syrup, sugar, and butter and bring to a simmer over low heat. Place the cereal in a large mixing bowl. Stir the corn syrup mixture into the cereal. Press in an even layer into the bottom and sides of the pie pan. Refrigerate until chilled, about 1 hour. (The crust may be cooled to room temperature, wrapped in plastic, and frozen for up to 1 month.)

2. Make the Filling: Place the cream cheese in a mixing bowl and beat with an electric mixer until fluffy. Add the sweetened condensed milk, espresso powder, and vanilla and mix until smooth, scraping down the sides of the bowl several times as necessary.

3. Pour the filling into the chilled crust. Cover with plastic and freeze until firm, at least 3 hours and up to 3 days.

4. Make the Warm Chocolate Sauce: Put 2 inches of water in a medium-size saucepan and bring the pot to a bare simmer. Combine the chocolate and water in a stainless-steel bowl big enough to rest on top of the saucepan and place the bowl over the simmering water, making sure that the water doesn't touch the bottom of the bowl. Heat the chocolate, whisking occasionally, until it is completely melted. Turn off the heat and stir in the liqueur, if desired. (The sauce can be refrigerated in an airtight container for up to 2 days. Reheat in a microwave oven for 1 $\frac{1}{2}$ minutes, or over a pot of simmering water before using.)

6. Slice the pie, and transfer slices to dessert plates. Pour some sauce over each slice and serve immediately.

# frosted flakes shortcakes with peaches and cream

The tender biscuits in this wonderful summer dessert get their crunch and a little sweetness from ground Frosted Flakes.

### SHORTCAKES

1 1/2 teaspoons grated orange zest

1/4 cup granulated sugar

1 1/4 cups Frosted Flakes (to make about 1/2 cup crumbs)

1 1/2 cups unbleached all-purpose flour

1 tablespoon baking powder

1/2 teaspoon salt

6 tablespoons (3/4 stick) unsalted butter, cut into 1/4-inch pieces and chilled

2/3 cup milk, plus 1 or 2 tablespoons more if necessary

### PEACHES

2 pounds peaches, peeled, pitted and cut into thick slices

1/3 cup granulated sugar

1/2 teaspoon vanilla extract

### WHIPPED CREAM

1 cup heavy cream, chilled

3 tablespoons confectioners' sugar

1. Preheat the oven to 400°F.
2. Make the Shortcakes: Combine the orange zest and granulated sugar in the work bowl of a food processor and process until the mixture is pale orange. Set aside.
3. Place the Frosted Flakes in the work bowl of the food processor (no need to wash it) and process until finely ground.
4. Combine the ground cereal, flour, baking powder, and salt in the bowl of an electric mixer and stir on low to combine. Add the butter and mix on low until the mixture resembles coarse meal. Add the milk and mix on low until the dough just comes together.

*(continued on page 106)*

5. Drop the dough in 6 mounds on a parchment-lined baking sheet. Sprinkle with the sugar and orange zest mixture. Bake until golden, 18 to 20 minutes. Slide the parchment onto a wire rack to let the biscuits cool.

6. Prepare the Peaches: In a bowl, combine the peaches, sugar, and vanilla and let stand, stirring occasionally, until the sugar has dissolved, about 15 minutes.

6. Make the Whipped Cream: Combine the cream and confectioners' sugar in the bowl of an electric mixer and whip until the cream just holds stiff peaks.

7. To assemble, use a sharp serrated knife to cut off the top third of each biscuit. Place each bottom on a dessert place. Spoon some peaches and their liquid on top of each biscuit. Spoon some of the whipped cream on top of the peaches. Replace the biscuit tops. Serve immediately.

# Menus for cereal fanatics

If you truly love cereal, you might want to cook up one of the following menus, each created with cereal recipes from this book:

## Italian Idyll
Pappa al Pomodoro, American Style • page 58
Italian-Style Meat Loaf with Semolina and Spinach • page 60
Creamy Espresso Pie with Cocoa Krispies Crust • pages 102–103

## Middle-Eastern Feast
Grape-Nuts Tabbouleh • page 48
Middle Eastern Lamb Meatballs with Pita Breads and Minted
    Yogurt Sauce • page 62
Pistachio ice cream and orange sorbet

## Special K Special
Caesar Salad with Special K Croutons • page 45
Turkey Burgers with Year-Round Tomato Salsa • pages 79–81
Secret Ingredient Oatmeal-Chip Cookies • page 90

## Weeknight Dinner with Holiday Flavors
Crisp Turkey Cutlets with Cranberry Pan Sauce • pages 76–78
Crispy Baked Sweet Potatoes • page 56
Apple Crisp with Cheerios and Almond Topping • page 96

# Index

Page numbers in *italic* indicate illustrations